W9-ADJ-709

Highland Ponies

by Grace Hansen

Abdo Kids Jumbo is an Imprint of Abdo Kids
abdobooks.com

abdobooks.com

Published by Abdo Kids, a division of ABDO, P.O. Box 398166, Minneapolis, Minnesota 55439. Copyright © 2020 by Abdo Consulting Group, Inc. International copyrights reserved in all countries. No part of this book may be reproduced in any form without written permission from the publisher. Abdo Kids Jumbo™ is a trademark and logo of Abdo Kids.

Printed in the United States of America, North Mankato, Minnesota.

052019

092019

 THIS BOOK CONTAINS
RECYCLED MATERIALS

Photo Credits: Alamy, Getty Images, iStock, Shutterstock

Production Contributors: Teddy Borth, Jennie Forsberg, Grace Hansen
Design Contributors: Dorothy Toth, Pakou Moua

Library of Congress Control Number: 2018963352
Publisher's Cataloging-in-Publication Data

Names: Hansen, Grace, author.

Title: Highland ponies / by Grace Hansen.

Description: Minneapolis, Minnesota : Abdo Kids, 2020 | Series: Horses set 2 |
    Includes online resources and index.

Identifiers: ISBN 9781532185649 (lib. bdg.) | ISBN 9781532186622 (ebook) |
    ISBN 9781532187117 (Read-to-me ebook)

Subjects: LCSH: Highland pony--Juvenile literature. | Horses--Juvenile
    literature.

Classification: DDC 636.16--dc23

Table of Contents

Highland Ponies

Highland ponies are native to Scotland. Their bloodlines can be traced to the 1830s. Then, they were used by small farmers to pull carts.

5

Today, they are still hardy horses. They are best used for carrying heavy loads over rough land.

A Highland pony is 13 to 14.2 **hands** tall. It has a strong, sturdy body.

9

Its head is supported by a strong neck. The pony's **muzzle** is short and ends in wide **nostrils**.

The breed has short legs.

Feathery, soft hair grows

on the backs of the legs.

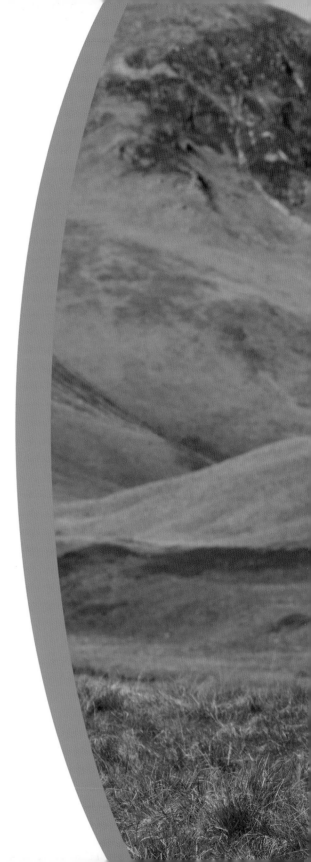

Highland ponies come in many colors, including black, brown, and bay. Many have stripes on their legs and spines.

Their manes and tails are often darker than their coats. The hair is flowy and usually left untrimmed.

Personality & Strength

Highlands make great family ponies. They are smart and docile. They can be trained for riding and showing.

Their strength is what makes
them good work ponies.
Many Highlands work on
farms in the hills of Scotland.

More Facts

- Highland ponies are easy to handle and easily trained.

- Highland ponies are one of the oldest horse breeds in Great Britain.

- This horse is **native** to the Scottish Highlands. So, it has grown to handle harsh and changing weather.

Glossary

bay – brown body color with black legs, mane, tail, and ears.

bloodline – an animal's direct set of ancestors.

docile – willing to obey rules and easy to manage.

hand – a unit of measurement of a horse's height, equal to 4 inches (10.16 cm).

muzzle – the part of the head of some animals that contains the nose, jaws, and mouth.

native – an animal found naturally in a given place.

nostrils – the two openings on the nose.

23

Index

Abdo Kids
ONLINE
FREE! ONLINE MULTIMEDIA RESOURCES

Visit abdokids.com to access crafts, games, videos, and more!

Use Abdo Kids code

HHK5649

or scan this QR code!